Animal Poems From A to Z

By Meish Goldish

SCHOLASTIC

PROFESSIONAL BOOKS

New York • Toronto • London • Auckland • Sydney

Cover art by J. Conteh Morgan
Interior illustration by Jan Pyk
Design by Frank Maiocco

ISBN 0-590-49741-3

Contents

Welcome to Animal Poems From A to Z. On the pages that follow, you'll find poetry about alligators, bears, cows, dogs, elephants, frogs, giraffes, horses, ladybugs, monkeys, penguins, rabbits, sharks, turtles, whales, zebras—whew!—and everything else in between.

Because children are naturally curious about the creatures that share their world, animal poetry provides wonderful opportunities to build literacy and to enrich thematic study. Of course, there is no one right way to present this collection of poems to your young learners. (After all, poetry is to be played with, and besides, you know your students best!) However, the following tips and guidelines can help you and your students make the most of this collection and your poetry sharing sessions.

Getting Started: The Poetry Corner

Almost any classroom nook or cranny can be dubbed a Poetry Corner. Even if one of your other learning centers such as your listening table or your library corner must do double-duty to accommodate such a center, it's worth the effort—poetry deserves a special spot of its own within the classroom.

Your poetry corner needn't be elaborate, but at minimum it needs to contain a scrapbook filled with copies of favorite poems, students' original poems displayed at their eye-level, and at least one bookshelf stocked with a permanent collection of poetry anthologies representing poems from around the world. To this basic setup you can add other items such as books on loan from students and the library, student-illustrated charts and commercially prepared posters featuring favorite poetic selections as well as poet profiles. You'll also want to include a small tape recorder (headphones not necessary if volume is kept low) along with a supply of poems on tape (check your library), plus a collection of student-made tapes. Finish off with a learning center label reading "Our Poetry Corner."

Sharing The Poems: Reading Poetry Aloud

Presenting the upbeat animal rhymes in this book can be as simple as reading them aloud whenever you have a chance. Lots of daily occasions call for one or more of these poems to be read aloud. Try them:

- as an early-morning starter
- as a late-afternoon wrap-up
- as a transition between two different curriculum areas
- as part of a mini-lesson before writing workshop time
- as one component of storytime
- as a poem-a-day read-aloud
- as a regular circle-time activity

Because these animal poems are rich with language, rhyme, repetition, and imagery, you can feel good just having children listen to them on a regular basis. Still, there will be times when you'll want to put these (and other) poems to work enhancing your curriculum—enriching your thematic studies, using them to teaching new skills, and relying on them to propel you and your students through any number of related classroom explorations.

Interactive Poetry Experiences

Beyond just reading these poems to your students, you'll want to get kids actively involved in the poetry experience. Here is a list of quick tips for helping the children "own" favorite poems:

One More Time

Repetition is the best way for children to effortlessly memorize a poem. While this doesn't mean you should "do a poem to death," it does mean that as long as student interest runs high, you can share the same poems again and again. For the same reasons children will request the same story or song over and over, they will enjoy hearing favorite animal poems repeated again and again. Once mastered and memorized, the poems will be theirs to pull and enjoy whenever they wish!

Call-A-Chant

With this singsong-y method, children learn to repeat each line of an animal poem (or any rhyming poem or song) after you. Children will really enjoy the rhythm and beat of this fail-safe method of repeating their best-loved animal poems. (Teaching Tip: Invite children to be your "echoes." Once skilled in response-chanting a particular poem, they can take turns acting as leader for the rest of the group.)

Take Note

Rhyming poems have many of the same elements as rhythmic songs—that's why you'll often observe little bodies swinging and swaying to the poetic beat. To make beautiful poetic music together, offer children rhythm instruments so they may tap, shake, clang and bang out the animal poem as they say it. No instruments on hand? Just use hands and feet to clap and stomp out the beat! Then try making up tunes to accompany the poems.

A "While-You're-At-It" Recording Session

When children are able to recite or call and chant a number of poems, use a tape recorder to record their efforts. Then place the tape in your Poetry Corner. Ask school faculty, staff, and administrators to record favorite animal poems. You may also send blank tapes and the recorder home with students so parents can make tapes of family favorites to share in class. Listening to other people read poetry has a big impact on children.

Poetry On Display

Charts

As part of a print-rich environment, children should see poems on display. One easy way to achieve this is to copy each animal poem onto one page of a large chart pad. It's best to copy the poem while the whole group looks on, as this provides one more language experience linking oral and aural language to the written language form. The charts may be illustrated by the children and can serve as poetic big books. If you wish to incorporate the poem charts into your reading instruction, they can provide a meaningful way for children to explore letters and letter sounds, rhyming words, repetitive words, and vocabulary, as well as poetic structures evident in the poems, such as similes (using *like* or *as* to make comparisons) and metaphors (or figures of speech).

Displays For Halls And Walls

You can easily incorporate the animal poems into bulletin board displays. For example, a copy of a poem may be printed in the center of the display surrounded by animal facts, illustrations, or student-generated poems. If you like, copies of the poems students learned in class may double as a bulletin board border (perhaps framing an animal mural) or may be hung side-by-side in the school hallway, thus providing a visual record of the animal poems presented in class. Copies of poems may also be glued to animal shapes created by the students and attached to a display with a tape hinge.

Readers' Theater Presentations

Animal poems are fun for children to read aloud in unison for an audience consisting of family members and/or other classes. Provide each student with a copy of the animal poems you will be reading together. Also, provide plenty of practice read-throughs to reduce anxiety. If you plan to divide the lines of poetry among groups of children, be sure to use highlighter to flag the lines each group will be reading. While all students can enjoy this "reading together aloud" experience, it is especially popular with children who would otherwise be reticent to share aloud in front of an audience. It's a real self-esteem booster!

Thematic Links

Shape Books

Make animal shape book materials and poems available for students to use when recording their own poems, stories, and research reports. First, refer students to this book's Table of Contents so they may choose a list of Top Ten Favorite Animals. Then draw or trace the outline of each animal shape (or face) and use this outline as a guide for cutting out animal-shaped booklet covers (from construction paper) and pages (from copy paper). Slip animal covers and pages into separate envelopes and place into your Poetry Corner, thematic center, or writing workshop area.

Take-Home Poems

When preparing thematic backpacks (filled with children's literature selections, parent resource books, and do-at-home activities), try tucking copies of related poems in, as well. Suggest that families read the poems together with their children. Challenge families to make poetry a regular part of their family reading time.

Cross-Curricular Activities

Sharing this collection of animal poems with your students will be a delight in itself. But, for those times when you want their learning to reach beyond the rhymes, we've included here a collection of poetry-inspired projects, games, crafts, and activities. These poetry follow-ups represent every area of the curriculum including writing, art, movement, music, science, and math. When browsing through these offerings, why not pick two or three and ask the children to decide for themselves which activity they'd like to try?

Collaborative Animal Anthology

Begin by dividing the class into cooperative pairs and having children look through animal resource books to locate favorite animals featured in the poems. Offer each pair of partners a set of drawing materials including pencils, erasers, markers, crayons, and lightweight copy paper. Suggest that the students experiment with tracing or drawing their favorite animals. When they are satisfied with their illustrations, offer each pair of students a large piece of oaktag on which to draw their finalized illustrations (allowing space beneath the drawings to add sentences about each animal). On separate pieces of copy or scrap paper, student teams can compose fun facts telling about each animal they have drawn. Encourage them to use information provided in the poem and to add information from their research.

After you have had a chance to help students edit their written work, have students transfer their sentences to the spaces below the illustrations. Make sure children sign their names to their work. When all polished pages are complete, compile them into a large class book. Pages may be arranged alphabetically by animal name, or grouped according to classification (mammals, birds, fish, etc.). Have children decide together on a title such as "Our Class Big Book of Animals." Write the title on an additional piece of oaktag. Ask for volunteers to create an illustration for the book's cover. Bind the pages together by using a hole punch and threading the holes with loose-leaf rings or yarn. (Teaching Tip: If you wish, make copies of the poems featuring the animals chosen by each pair of children and paste them on the page opposite the children's work.)

Pantomime Games And Play

Read or recite the animal poems aloud and invite volunteers to perform pantomimes of animals. As a poetry follow-up, children may prefer to take turns pantomiming favorite animals for classmates to guess or suggest that children make animal sounds for classmates to identify.

You may also provide simple props for pantomime play. Children will enjoy creating costumes from old clothing, sheets, blankets, masks, and other materials. If you like, provide paper headbands (for attaching paper ears), water-soluble eyebrow pencil (for drawing on whiskers) and brown grocery sacks (which may be painted for animal masks). Also, ask parents and colleagues to lend any animal costumes they may have stored away. In addition, provide students with time to practice acting out a poem or a familiar animal story, to make up an original tale about their animals, and then to perform a pantomime play for the rest of the class. Later, audience members can summarize the story based on the actions they viewed in the pantomimes.

Animal Collages And Mobiles

Have the class cut out pictures of animals from magazines and newspapers. Then supply children with large sheets of cardboard or oaktag. Let them organize their pictures into thematic collages. For example, they might make collages showing animals on land, animals in the water, and animals in the air. Or, they might make a reptile collage, a mammal collage, a bird collage, a fish collage, or an insect collage. If you wish, in the center of each collage glue a copy of a corresponding animal poem. Display the collages prominently in the classroom.

Children may create mobiles by gluing pictures of individual animals on pieces of paper or cardboard. On the reverse side of the cardboard, glue a copy of a corresponding animal poem. Punch a small hole at the top of each picture. Thread and knot yarn through each hole. Then hang the animals from a hanger or long rod suspended from the ceiling. Children might make a mobile of a school of fish or of birds flying through the skies, for example.

Information Charts And Cards

Use large sheets of oaktag or chart paper to create informational wall charts about the animals in the poems. On the charts, children enter information about each animal: what it looks like, where it lives, what it eats, how it moves, how it protects itself, and so on. Information may be taken from the poems or from additional reading sources. Expand the chart over a period of time as more information is gathered about the animals.

Children can also make their own animal information cards, similar to baseball cards. Using cardboard about the size of an index card, children draw a picture of an animal on one side of the card. On the other side, they list facts about the animal: its home, habitat, food, movement, and other details. Place all the cards in a large shoe box where children can read them in their free time.

Animal Poems And Songs

Invite children to write original poems and songs about their favorite animals. For poems, children may follow the same rhythms and rhyme schemes used in poems in the book, or they may create their own. For songs, children can create their own melodies, or base new songs on familiar tunes and lyrics.

Once the poems and songs are completed, encourage volunteers to perform their poems and songs live or to record them on tapes. Children may wish to prepare sound effects to accompany their poems and songs.

Habitat Murals And Models

Supply children with long sheets of brown or white butcher paper so they may create murals showing different kinds of habitats for animals. Children first draw pictures of each animal's type of home on the mural, such as a den, a hollow log, a bird's nest, a pond, a treetop or a hole in the ground. (For younger children, you may want to draw a ground line and a background suggesting a habitat.) Then ask children to add to the mural by drawing pictures of the individual animals in their habitats. They can further embellish the setting by gluing or taping leaves, twigs, grass, pebbles, and other nature items to the mural.

Children may also enjoy working together to build habitat models. Using a large empty pizza box or cardboard box as a base, each child fills the area with items necessary to make a comfortable habitat for a particular kind of animal. The habitat may include rocks, wood, leaves, grass, or other natural items. Children may fashion animals out of clay or use toy animals to complete each setting.

Animal Jigsaws

Have each child locate and clip a large picture of an animal from a magazine. (Discarded nature magazines are perfect for this!) Have children then glue each picture onto a piece of cardboard or oaktag. After the pictures have dried, have children draw three or four straight or wavy lines crisscrossing on the back of the cardboard. (You will have to supervise this part of the project to make certain children do not draw lines that result in jigsaw pieces that are too small.) Have children cut along the lines they have drawn. Pair each child with a partner. Have one child scramble a set of puzzle pieces, picture side up, on a tabletop and the other tries to guess the animal just by looking at the pieces. Then have them see how long it takes the partners to piece the puzzle together. They can take turns scrambling and guessing.

Animal Observation Logs

Ask each child to find an animal to observe each day over a period of time, such as a week. Children might observe a home pet such as a dog, cat, or fish, for example. Or they might watch a backyard animal such as a squirrel, bird, or ant. Tell children to keep a written log in which they note the animal's movement, behavior, and other habits. They should note details such as: time, date, and place of each visit; description of animal movements; any animal actions repeated over and over; animal reactions to stimuli such as food, noise, other people or other animals; etc. Set aside a regular time to encourage children to share their logs with the rest of the class. Ask children to tell any new information they were surprised to learn about and what they plan to observe next time out.

Puppet Plays

Animal puppets can be made from old white socks. Children may use colored markers to draw facial details on the socks. They may also embellish the puppets by using a hot glue gun (adult use only) to affix buttons for eyes, pipe cleaners for whiskers, or felt for a tongue. When all puppets are finished, encourage children to give each animal puppet a voice to describe life as an animal.

Animal Fantasies And Riddles

Encourage children to make up fantasy stories about animals. You might offer the following "what if" story starters to get children's creative juices flowing:

- If I were a ____, here's how I'd spend my day.
- If a ___ raced a ___, here's what might happen.
- If a giant ___ showed up in my home, I'd...
- If a ___ could talk with me, here's what we might say.

Children will also have fun making up animal riddles for classmates to try to answer. Give an example such as the following:

I have four legs.
I like to graze in a pasture.
I can give you something good to drink.
What am I? (a cow)

Invite children to read their riddles aloud and see how many classmates guess the answer correctly.

Pet Survey

Have children conduct a class or schoolwide survey to find out which animals are the most popular pets. Children should ask students about pets that they now have or had in the past. After all responses are tallied, the results can be presented in the form of a bar graph such as the one below. Then have children refer to the graph to locate information such as:

- *Which animal is the most popular pet?*
- *Which animal is the least popular pet?*
- *How many more students have dogs than cats?*
- *Which animal do 15 students have as a pet?*

Pet Presentations

Invite children who have pets to bring in pictures and make brief classroom presentations describing how they care for their pets at home. Ask them to describe what the pet is fed, how often it eats, where it sleeps, what its habits are, and so on. Children who don't have pets may enjoy preparing similar presentations on pets they wish they could own.

If possible, have pet owners take turns bringing their pets to class. At the end of each presentation, encourage audience members to ask questions they may have about the pet and its care. (Teaching Tip: Schedule a time first thing in the day for pet visitations. This way, a parent or family member may bring the pet to school, stay for the discussion and display [in order to help manage the pet] and then take the pet home immediately following the visit, if you wish.)

Animal Poems From A to Z

Animals From A To Z

A is Ape, B is Bee,
C is Clownfish in the sea!

D is Deer, E is Eel,
F's a Fox who wants a meal.

G is Goose, H is Hog,
I's an Inchworm on a log.

Jay is J, Koala's K,
L's a Lion far away.

M is Mule, N is Newt,
O's an Ostrich tall and cute.

P is Pig, Q is Quail,
R's a Rat with curly tail.

Snake is S, Turkey's T,
U's the Umbrella bird flying free.

V is Viper, Worm is W,
Birds' X are hatching. (Does that joke trouble you?)

Yak is Y, Zebra's Z,
Alphabet animals for you and me!

Alligator

Alligator, alligator, long as can be,
You look like a giant lizard to me!
Swimming in the swamp, with very sharp teeth,
Eyes above the water and jaw beneath.
Alligator, alligator, here's what we'll do:
I'll keep my mouth shut, and you should, too!

Anteater

Anteater, anteater,
Can't eat plants.
Anteater, anteater,
Can eat ants!

Anteater, anteater,
Stick out your tongue.
Anteater, anteater,
Look what has clung!

Anteater, anteater,
Under your snout
The ants go in
But don't come out!

Ants

The ants are marching in a row,
Ants! Ants! Ants! Ants!
In their colony, off they go!
Ants! Ants! Ants! Ants!
Army ants go out for prey,
Ants! Ants! Ants! Ants!
Harvester ants store seeds all day!
Ants! Ants! Ants! Ants!
Honey ants eat honeydew,
Ants! Ants! Ants! Ants!
Carpenter ants find wood to chew!
Ants! Ants! Ants! Ants!
Amazon ants, and fire ants!
Janitor ants, and bulldog ants!
Ants in picnics, ants in plants!
Ants! Ants! ANTS! ANTS!

Ape

Which animal is most like us in shape?
The ape!
Its arms and legs, its muscle and bone
Are much like our own!
Perhaps in the zoo you've had a glimpse
Of orangutans, gibbons, gorillas, and chimps.
These are the types of apes you'll find,
And each is a special kind!
Of animals of all sizes and shapes,
You're bound to go ape over apes!

Armadillo

The armadillo isn't soft like a pillow.
Its body is bony and hard.
The plates on its skin
Form a shell to curl in
If you try to catch it off guard.

Armadillos don't fight, they just roll up tight
In a very hard, very stiff ball.
And there they stay fast
Until danger has passed,
And then they come out to crawl.

Baby Animals

Oh, baby, baby, so young and so tame,
Oh, baby, baby, so what is your name?
Baby cow is a calf,
Baby deer is a fawn,
Baby goat is a kid eating grass on the lawn.
Baby bear is a cub,
Baby hen is a chick,
Baby swan is a cygnet so graceful and quick.
Baby goose is a gosling,
Baby seal is a pup,
Baby cat is a kitten drinking milk from a cup.
Baby sheep is a lamb,
Baby turkey's a poult,
Baby horse is a foal or a filly or colt.
Oh, baby, baby, so young and so tame,
Oh, baby, baby, be proud of your name!

Bats

Spooky bats go flying at night,
Flapping about in the pale moonlight.
Spreading their wings, they're a scary sight!
But truth be told, there's no need for fright.

Spooky bats are really not bad.
They eat harmful insects, for which we're glad!
They're somewhat shy, I might also add.
(But never grab one—it could get mad!)

Spooky bats like to sleep in the day.
They hang upside down and doze that way!
Caves and trees are where they stay,
Until it grows dark—then it's up and away!

Bear

Bear, bear, bear, bear!
How many kinds of bears are there?
Polar bear and grizzly bear,
Big brown bear with lots of hair!
Spectacled bear, black bear, too,
Sloth bear, sun bear, quite a few!
Bear, bear, bear, bear!
So many bears to compare!

Beaver

Busy, busy beaver,
Gnawing on a tree,
Chewing round the trunk
Till it falls down free.

Busy, busy beaver,
Working till it's dark.
Gnawing at the branches,
Chewing off the bark.

Busy, busy beaver,
Building up a home.
Hauling logs and leaves
And shaping a dome.

Busy, busy beaver,
Gnaw and chew and haul.
Of all the busy animals,
You're busiest of all!

Bee

BUZZ! goes the bee,
Hour after hour,
BUZZ! goes the bee
From flower to flower.

Sucking out the nectar,
Flying it home.
Storing up the nectar
In the honeycomb!

BUZZ! goes the bee,
Making honey so sweet.
Bee makes the honey
That I love to eat!

Big Brown Bear

Big brown bears are in the woods
Where they like to roam.
All the day they hunt and play
And make a cozy home.

Big brown bears are by the stream,
Lunch is what they wish.
With teeth and paws and sharpened
claws,
They plan to catch a fish!

Big brown bears are in their caves,
Where sleeping is their "thing."
They hibernate all winter long
And wake up in the spring!

Birds

Birds in the sky, in the lake, in the tree,
So many birds for you to see!
Mockingbird, blue jay, robin, sparrow,
Cardinal, oriole, swift as an arrow!
Bobolink, chickadee, bullfinch, crow,
Warbler, raven, watch them go!
Meadowlark, blackbird, nightingale, thrush,
Birds in a bush, and birds in the brush.
Woodpecker, hummingbird, osprey, owl,
Chicken and turkey (known as *fowl*).
Duck in the water, dove in the sky,
Ostrich and penguin, which don't even fly!
Swan and pelican, puffin and goose,
Buzzard and eagle on the loose.
Stork and heron with long thin legs,
Hawk and falcon, guarding their eggs.
Albatross, vulture, peacock, pheasant,
Birds that are wild, birds that are pleasant.
Birds in the sky, in the lake, in the tree,
So many birds for you to see!

Blue Whale

Wow, what a whale!
I can't believe my eyes!
Of all the living creatures,
It's the biggest in size.

Blue whale in the ocean
Swims anywhere it wishes.
Moving in the water,
Look out, little fishes!

Blue whale is hungry,
And what a mouth to fill!
Dining on its favorite treat:
Seafood called *krill*.

Blue whale in the ocean,
Blue whale in the sea.
Of all living creatures,
It's the biggest there can be!

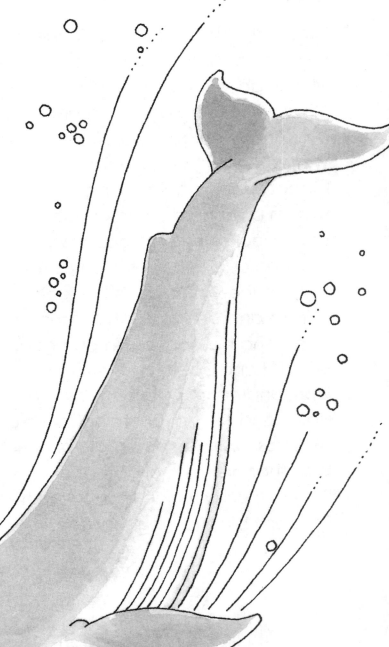

Bug

Ugh! A bug is under my rug!
Now it's on the floor.
Now it's crawling across the room,
Now it's out the door!

Butterflies

Butterflies go fluttering by
On colored wings that catch the eye.
On wings of orange, and silvery blue,
On wings of golden yellow, too.
Butterflies float in the air,
Making their homes most anywhere:
The rainforest, field, and prairie land,
On mountaintops, and desert sand.
If winter brings the cold and snow,
To warmer climates, off they go!
Returning home the following spring,
Beautiful butterflies on the wing!

Camel

In deserts, there wanders a mammal.
I'm speaking, of course, of the camel.
It's known for its humps
(Which store fat in lumps)
And for very sharp teeth of enamel!

The camel can haul a huge load
In places where there is no road.
And for weeks in the heat
When there's nothing to eat,
It survives in its desert abode!

Cat

My cat loves to purr
And gently lick her golden fur.
My cat sings "Meow!"
When eating fish and chicken chow!
My cat sharpens her claws
But not on the couch. (She knows the laws!)
My cat likes to nap,
And falls asleep right in my lap!
My cat acts purr-fectly
So there's never a cat-astrophe!

Cheetah

The cheetah is a very swift cat,
Running the plains in no time flat.
It's five times faster than a flying bat.
Now what, oh what, do you think of that?

The cheetah's body is covered with spots.
Its yellow coat has dark black dots.
And when it slowly walks or trots,
You'll see those spots are lots and lots!

Chicken

Known for its feathers and wings and legs,
The chicken lays eggs and eggs and eggs!
Known for the comb atop its crown,
The chicken lays eggs of white and brown.
Known for its strut when taking a walk,
The chicken lays eggs! Ba-a-awk! Ba-a-awk!

Chipmunk

Hop, skip! Hop, skip! Hop, skip, skip!
Chipmunk's off on a hunting trip.
Hunting for nuts, hunting for seeds,
Hunting for all its winter needs.
Storing the crops in a tunnel below,
Then staying indoors during winter's snow.
Skip, hop! Skip, hop! Skip, hop, hop!
Smart little chipmunk, store your crop!

Clam

On the ocean floor,
The clam's in its shell,
And there it's protected
Very well!

Cow

How come a cow
Never says "Ow!"
Whenever there's milking to do?
It doesn't say "Ow!"
For it pleases the cow,
So instead, the cow says "Moo!"

Crocodile

The crocodile
Has a toothy smile.
His teeth are sharp and long.
And in the swamp
When he takes a chomp,
His bite is quick and strong!

So if you smile
At a crocodile,
There's just one thing I'll say:
If he smiles too,
Be sure that you
Are very far away!

Deer

Deer are roaming in the grass,
In the field I watch them pass.
Deer are grazing on the loose,
Reindeer, red deer, elk, and moose.
Deer with antlers tall and wide,
Royal horns that are worn with pride.
Deer are precious things to see,
Deer are very dear to me.

Defenses

What do animals do to defend
Themselves from those who aren't a friend?
Sharks bite with deadly jaws.
Kangaroos kick with sharpened claws.
Porcupines stab with pointed quills.
Woodpeckers peck with powerful bills.
Moose use horns when caught in a fight.
Snakes rely on their poisonous bite.
Clams shut up inside their shell.
Opossums play dead, and do it well.
Rabbits hop away very fast.
Electric eels give a shocking blast!
Octopuses shoot an ugly ink,
And skunks will make an awful stink!
Chameleons hide in the grass or trees.
Their colors blend in, so no one sees.
Gophers race to a hole in the ground,
And birds fly away when there's danger around.
Running or hiding or fighting back,
There are many defenses in case of attack!

Dog

Ruff, ruff! Bow wow!
My dog's a super pet, and how!
With floppy ears and wagging tail,
He loves to run and fetch the mail!
I toss a bone that's smooth and hard,
He buries it in our backyard!
He's friendly in the neighborhood,
Our neighbors say he's *doggone* good!
He loves to leap so playfully
And chases squirrels up a tree.
Ruff, ruff! Meow, meow!
Guess who my dog is chasing now!

Dogs Around The World

Spin the globe, and you will find
Homelands for dogs of every kind:
English setters, Irish hounds,
Labrador retrievers making rounds.
Siberian huskies pulling a sled,
Mexican chihuahuas raised and bred.
German shepherds herding a flock,
Australian cattle dogs guarding stock.
American foxhounds following game,
Norwegian elkhounds doing the same.
Scottish terriers, Chinese pugs,
Japanese akitas with serious mugs!
Spin the globe, wherever you go,
You're bound to find a dog you know!

Dolphin

What sets dolphins apart?
They're very smart!
What makes dolphins first-rate?
They communicate!
How do dolphins "speak"?
They click, whistle, and squeak!
How was this information found?
By recording their sound!

Duck

Duck in the water, quack, quack, quack!
Soft, white feathers on your back, back, back!
Duck in the water, splash and splish!
Dip in your bill and catch those fish!

Duck out of water, walk on land.
Your webbed feet make it hard to stand!
Waddle with your family, waddle in a pack.
Duck out of water, quack, quack, quack!

Eagle

The eagle is a noble bird
With features bald and bold.
It soars with pride
On wings so wide,
With beak and claws of gold.

The eagle is our nation's bird,
Flying proud and free.
If I could fly
Up in the sky,
An eagle's what I'd be!

Electric Eel

Never feel
An electric eel.
It's no fun
To receive its stun!

Elephant

The elephant surely is grand!
It's the largest creature on land!
With jumbo-sized ears,
No wonder it hears
For miles from where it may stand.

The elephant surely is great!
Over five tons is its weight!
With jumbo-sized feet,
Plus a mouth that can eat
More than 700 pounds on its plate!

The elephant surely is strong!
With ivory tusks sharp and long!
And the heaviest chunk
It can lift with its trunk!
Yes, an elephant just can't go wrong!

Extinct Animals

Extinct animals no longer survive.
Not one of their kind is now alive.
Once, for example, dinosaurs were here,
Until each one seemed to disappear.
The dodo bird, the mammoth, too,
And the passenger pigeon are just a few
Of extinct animals who live no more.
They've taught us a lesson we can't ignore:
Let's care for the animals living today,
Don't take their homes or their shelters away!
Show them respect, and help them to last
So extinct animals are a thing of the past!

Fireflies

Glowing, glowing in the night,
Fireflies shine a yellow light.
Flashing signals to their mates,
Such a bright sight each creates!
Glowing, glowing in the night,
Fireflies shine a yellow light.

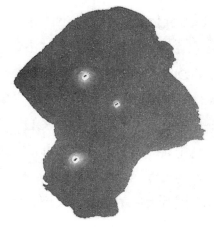

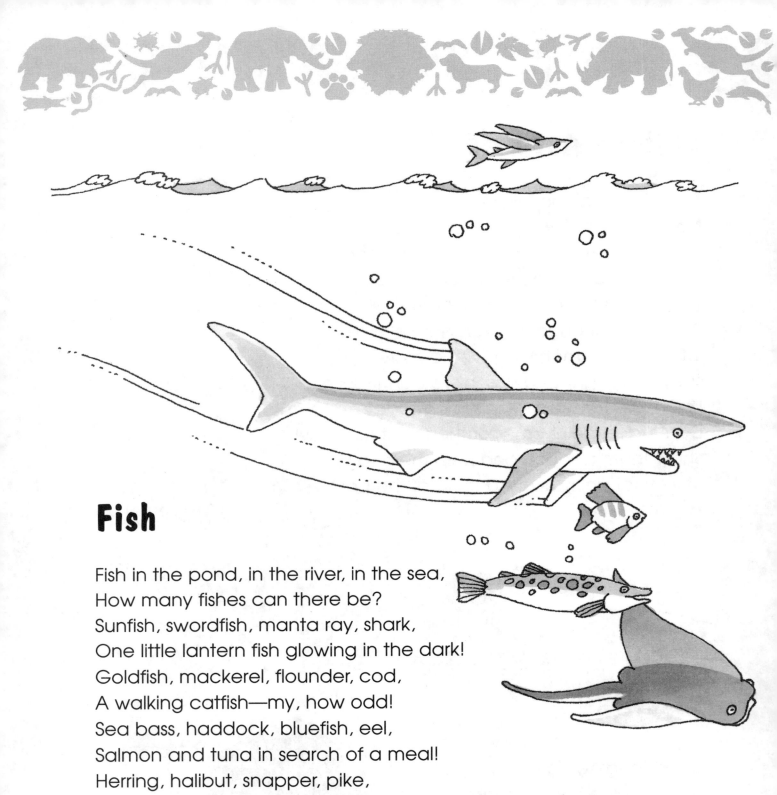

Fish

Fish in the pond, in the river, in the sea,
How many fishes can there be?
Sunfish, swordfish, manta ray, shark,
One little lantern fish glowing in the dark!
Goldfish, mackerel, flounder, cod,
A walking catfish—my, how odd!
Sea bass, haddock, bluefish, eel,
Salmon and tuna in search of a meal!
Herring, halibut, snapper, pike,
Barracuda swift and ready to strike!
Angelfish, flatfish, kingfish, trout,
Flying fish in the water leaping out!
Sailfish, sturgeon, sardine, shad,
Thousands of fish—now that's not bad!

Fish In Schools

Schools aren't only for kids like you,
Schools can be for fishes, too!
Fish are in schools, but not for reading!
Schools for fish are for swimming and breeding.
A school of fish means fish in a group.
A school is a crowd, a school is a troop.
Schools may be large, or schools may be small.
(And some fish don't live in schools at all!)
A tuna school might number twenty,
A herring school could have millions—that's plenty!
Fish in a school stay side by side,
Helping keep enemies away as they glide.
If going to school is your fondest wish,
You'd *still* get to do it if you were a fish!

Flamingo

What kind of bird has legs like sticks,
And long pink feathers soft and thick?
What kind of bird has a neck like an **S**?
What kind of bird? Go ahead—take a guess:
BINGO!
It's the flamingo!

What kind of bird spends its day near a lake,
And has a long bill for food to take?
What kind of bird can be five feet high?
What kind of bird? Go ahead—take a try:
BINGO!
It's the flamingo!

Flea

Teeny, tiny flea!
As tiny as can be!
Teeny as a tiny pinch,
Measuring only an eighth of an inch,
But, oh, its bite can make you flinch!
Teeny, tiny flea!

Fly

A fly flies by, quicker than the eye!
On two thin wings, it darts up high.
Those tiny wings can really fly!
Beating 200 times a second—oh, my!
The fly goes BUZZ! as it flaps in the sky.
The BUZZ! you hear are the wings going by!
So if a fly ever catches your eye,
Don't ask why it buzzes—you now know why!

Fox

Oh so clever, oh so sly,
A small red fox goes dashing by.
Very wily, very cunning,
In a flash it's off and running.
By the river, by the den,
In its fox hole, out again!
Racing up and racing down,
Now the fox trots off to town!
In the woods near trees and rocks,
There's a nifty, shifty fox!

Frog

Frog on a lily pad! Frog on a log!
Leap, frog! Leap, frog! Leap, leap, frog!
First a tadpole, or baby frog,
Also known as a polliwog!

Growing bigger, hopping about,
Losing its tail as its legs grow out.
Looking around with bulging eyes,
Using its tongue to catch those flies!

Splash in the water, get a good soak.
Stretch the hind legs, start to stroke!
Sing your song, frog! Sing for the folk!
Ribbit, ribbit, ribbit! Croak, croak, croak!

Giant Panda

The giant panda looks like a bear,
Black and white, with fuzzy hair.
The giant panda is very rare,
It can't be found just anywhere.
It lives in Asia in a mountain lair,
And eats the bamboo growing there.
Giant panda, please take care!
It's true that you're beyond compare!

Giraffe

Of all the animals walking tall,
The giraffe's the tallest of them all!
Its body stretches very high,
With legs much longer than you or I!
(A giraffe standing on your kitchen floor
Would be three times taller than the door!)
Its legs are long, but if you check,
You'll find an even longer neck!
The neck helps to reach leaves high on a tree,
Leaves other creatures can't even see!
With such a long neck, I'd like to note:
Pity the giraffe with a sore throat!

Gnu

Hi there, gnu,
What's gnu with you?
You look so sad.
You look so blue.
Is there anything
I can do?

Goat

What bearded animal helps on the farm?
The goat!
What friendly creature is loaded with charm?
The goat!
Who can produce both milk and wool?
The goat!
Who grows long horns like a bull?
The goat!
What creature can mow your lawn,
Eating the grass until it's gone?
What animal can you always count on?
The goat!

Goldfish

Bright, pretty goldfish,
With colors so bold.
Bright yellow-orange
Like a band of gold!

Bright, pretty goldfish,
A sight to behold.
Bright yellow-orange
Like a band of gold!

Grasshopper

Hop! Hop! Hop!
My, what strength!
A grasshopper hops
Twenty times its length!
Hop in the grass
On a single blade,
Hop in the sun,
Or hop in the shade.
Farmer says, "Grasshopper,
Stay off my crop!"
There goes the grasshopper,
Hop! Hop! Hop!

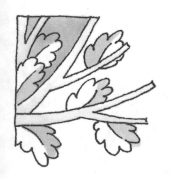

Habitats

Home, sweet home!
Home, sweet animal home!
Birds like to rest
In a twiggy nest.
A big brown bear
Prefers a lair.
Bats love to rave
About their cave!
Monkeys swing free
High in a tree!
The tiny frog
Lives on a log.
Chipmunks are found
In a hole in the ground.
Home in a thicket?
A lion would pick it!
The crab lives well
In an empty shell.
A hive will please
A family of bees.
Is *your* home the home
For dogs or cats?
Animals have many habitats!

Helpers

Did you ever stop and try to recall
The ways that animals help us all?
Bees give us honey, cows give us milk,
Chickens give eggs, and silkworms silk.
Sheep give us wool we make into clothes,
Animals help us in ways like those!
Dogs guide the blind, and some herd sheep,
While others guard homes while we're fast asleep.
Horses give rides on country roads,
And mules help farmers pull heavy loads.
Animals are pets, like a bird or a cat,
Animals help us in ways like that!

Hermit Crab

Hermit crab, you live all alone
In an empty shell in the sea.
With all those fish,
Don't you ever wish
For a little company?

Hippopotamus

Hip, hip, hooray!
The hippo's here to stay!
Its size astounds:
Over 5,000 pounds!
Now that's a *lot* to weigh!

Horse

Who gallops swiftly down the lane,
Slowing to a trot when I pull the rein?
Who has a pony tail and a mane?
Of course—it's my horse!

Who loves to jump and leap and bound,
Stomping its hooves upon the ground?
Who likes to play and horse around?
Of course—it's my horse!

Who nibbles oats and piles of hay?
Who has a stable where to stay?
Who likes to whinny and just say "Neigh"?
Of course—it's my horse!

Hummingbird

Hum! goes the hummingbird,
Hum! Hum! Hum!
Hummingbird, tiny as my
Thumb! Thumb! Thumb!
Up, down, back and forth,
Go and come!
The flapping of its wings makes the
Hum! Hum! Hum!

Inchworm

The inchworm crawls
An inch at a time.
The inchworm is short
And so is this rhyme!

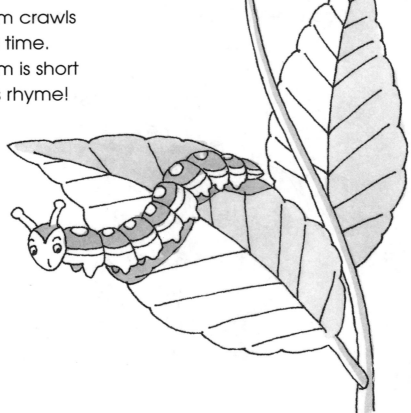

Jellyfish

I know that there are jellyfish,
But tell me if it's true:
Could there also be
In the sea
Peanut-butter fish, too?

June Bug

June bug, June bug,
Please reply:
What do they call you
In July?

Kangaroo

How do you do, kangaroo?
You seem so very hoppy.
You hop hop here,
You hop hop there,
With tail that's stiff, not floppy.

How do you do, kangaroo?
You're hoppy, not a grouch.
You hop hop here,
You hop hop there,
With baby joey in your pouch!

How do you do, kangaroo,
You roam throughout Australia.
You hop hop here,
You hop hop there,
So fast that I can't tail ya'!

Katydid

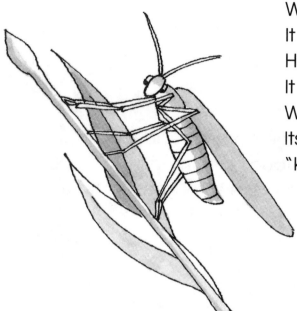

What did the katydid do?
It sang the whole night through!
How did the katydid sing?
It rubbed wing against wing.
Why did the katydid get its name?
Its song sounds the same:
"Katydid-katydid! Katydid-katydid!"

Koala

Who's in Australia? The koala is there.
It looks a lot like a teddy bear.
Sleeping all day in the eucalyptus tree,
At night it climbs out and then roams free.
Koalas don't drink any water, it's true.
So when they're thirsty, what do they do?
They claw at tree leaves to pry them loose,
Then chew the leaves, and drink the juice!

Ladybug

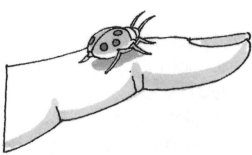

The ladybug's a beetle.
It's shaped like half a pea.
Its color is a bright red
With lots of spots to see.

Although the name is "ladybug,"
Some ladybugs are "men."
So why don't we say "gentleman bug"
Every now and then?

Land, Sea, And Air Animals

Animals that crawl or stand
Mostly live upon the land.
Animal with fins and tail
Love the water, where they sail.
Animals with wings will fly
High up in the open sky.
So if you're playing hide and seek
With some animal friends this week,
Remember three places to look with care:
On land, on sea, and in the air!

Laughing Hyena

Hi, hyena!
What do you say?
You seem to be laughing a lot today!
Hi, hyena,
Out on the prowl.
I hear your laugh is really a howl!

Leopard

Leaping leopard in a tree,
Graceful a cat as there could be.
Leaping leopard, down you climb,
Making your way in record time.
Leaping leopard, hiding in the grass,
Waiting to pounce as animals pass!

Lion

The lion is the king of beasts,
It has a mighty roar.
It eats a meal
And then will rest
For twenty hours or more!

The lion roams the grassy plain
With members of its pride.
They sleep and play
Throughout the day
All staying side by side.

The lion is a royal beast,
Its mane is thick and long.
I can't think of
Another beast
More beautiful or strong!

Lizard

Lizard in the desert,
Lizard on the ground,
Lizard climbing rocks
And scampering around.

Chameleon's a lizard,
So is the iguana.
If you could be a lizard,
Do you think you'd wanna?

Llama

The llama's like
A camel a lot.
But camels have humps
While llamas do not!

The llama's name
Is tricky to spell:
Remember to start
With an extra **L**!

Lobster

The lobster has five pairs of legs,
The first four are for walking.
But the fifth, instead,
Is in front of its head,
For catching food it is stalking!

The lobster has five pairs of legs,
But here's some happy news:
With such large claws
It's lucky because
It doesn't have to wear shoes!

Mice

If grown-ups are strong,
And mice are weak,
Why do mice
Make grown-ups say "Eek!"?

Migration

In wintertime, many an animal moves
To a warmer place till the weather improves.
This yearly change of one's location
Is known as *seasonal migration*.
Birds up north fly south on the wing.
Returning home when it's warms in the spring.
Whales seek warmer waters for breeding,
Then later swim to cold waters for feeding!
When monarch butterflies feel chilly weather,
They fly south for 2,000 miles together!
Perhaps *you've* gone south to stay warm for a spell:
Yes, people are animals who migrate as well!

Mockingbird

Mockingbird, mockingbird,
How well you mock!
You imitate other birds
'Round the clock.

Mockingbird, mockingbird,
Hearing their song.
Learning the sounds
And then singing out strong!

Monkey

In the forest, in a tree,
There's a monkey swinging free.
Hanging by his hands and feet,
Looking for a treat to eat.
Ripe bananas grow nearby,
Soon they've caught the monkey's eye.
Monkey grabs one, starts to peel,
Now he's got a monkey meal!

Mosquito

Pesky mosquito,
Please fly away!
The buzzing in my ear
Is spoiling my day!

Moth

The tiny moth
Can eat through cloth,
So here's some good advice:
For clothes you store
In a closet or drawer,
Use mothballs to keep them nice!

Mouse

A tiny mouse
Came inside my house,
Through a tiny crack in the floor.
It stole some cheese
Without saying "Please"
And then scampered out the door!

Movement

How does an animal get around?
On foot it sometimes moves.
A dog with paws,
A cat with claws,
A cow and a horse with hooves.

How does an animal get about
When flying in the sky?
The bird and the bat
Flap wings where they're at,
Then go sailing by.

How does an animal get along
When swimming in the sea?
With fins and a tail
A fish will sail,
And with flippers, a whale moves free.

With paws and claws and feathers and fins,
Animals get around.
As for you and me,
We move about, free
With our feet firmly on the ground!

Mule

Cross a donkey
with a horse
And you'll End up with a mule,
Of course!

Nightingale

Nightingale, nightingale,
Timid and shy,
Rapidly hopping along.
Nightingale, nightingale,
Timid and shy,
Singing your beautiful song.

Octopus

The arms on the octopus number eight:
One, two, three, four, five, six, seven, eight!
All curled up, then pointing straight,
One, two, three, four, five, six, seven, eight!
In the ocean, octopuses wait,
One, two, three, four, five, six, seven, eight,
For clams and crabs to put on their plate!
One, two, three, four, five, six, seven, eight!

Opossum

The opossum is loving, and never a grouch.
She carries her babies around in a pouch.
The babies grow bigger, but stay by her side.
They climb on her back and she gives them a ride!

The opossum is clever, and hunts in the night.
Her very sharp teeth make it easy to bite.
And if she's in danger, she uses her head
By lying quite still and pretending she's dead!

Ostrich

Do you know the world's largest bird?
Aw—it's the ostrich!
What bird is eight feet tall? My word!
Aw—it's the ostrich!
Who moves fifteen feet in a single step?
Who runs forty miles an hour with pep?
Who roars like a lion, hisses like a snake,
And weighs 300 pounds, for heaven's sake?
Aw—it's the ostrich!

Owl

The owl, they say, is a wise old bird.
It only asks a single word:
"Who? Who? Who? Who?"
Perched upon a branch so high,
It never asks "What?" or "Where?" or "Why?"
Just "Who? Who? Who? Who?"

Parrots

Red and blue and orange and green,
Parrots have feathers like you've never seen!
The white-feathered cockatoo's a friendly fellow,
Wearing a beautiful crown of yellow!
The scarlet macaw is a bird to hail
With an orange-red, long, and very straight tail!
The rainbow lorikeet flies quite high
And looks like a rainbow in the sky!
Red and blue and orange and green,
Parrots have feathers like you've never seen!

Penguin

The penguin's a bird that cannot fly
But can swim like a torpedo!
And on the ice
It looks so nice
Dressed in its own tuxedo!

Pig

Behold the pig!
It's very big!
Its color pink
Is nice, I think!
Its tail's a beaut,
So curly cute!
And on the farm,
It oinks with charm!

Polar Bear

Brrr! Brrr! Polar bear,
Living on the ice.
Your bright, white furry coat
Keeps you warm and nice.

Brrr! Brrr! Polar bear,
Swimming in the sea.
In the freezing waters
You're as happy as can be!

Porcupine

Beware the porcupine! Beware!
Its back and sides have hard, stiff hair.
The hairs are quills quite sharp and strong,
So enemies will move along!
Some good advice with you I'll share:
Beware the porcupine! Beware!

Rabbit

For the rabbit, give three cheers!
One for its long and furry ears!
Two for its short and fluffy tail!
Three for its hop-hop down the trail!
For the rabbit, give three cheers!
Quick! Before it disappears!

Raccoon

Good afternoon, raccoon!
There's something I'd like to ask:
Why do you have those rings on your tail
And why do you wear a mask?

Good afternoon, raccoon!
There's something I'd like to say:
Why do you hunt for food at night
And stay in your den all day?

Rainforest Animals

Where can you find a toucan?
In the rainforest, *you* can!
High on a limb is where it
Can be seen with the monkey and parrot.
Squirrels leap from tree to tree,
While bats go flying free.
There's a bee, mosquito, and moth,
Look up! See the hanging sloth!
Down on the rainforest floor
Are big and small creatures galore:
The antelope, deer, and hog,
Plus termites and ants on a log.
Every day, hour by hour,
Butterflies float on a flower.
Lizards and snakes also play
In rainforest plants all day.
Ocelots, jaguars, leopards—yes!
The rainforest is a popular address!

Rattlesnake

Rattle, rattle, rattlesnake,
Rattle on the ground.
Beware if there's a rattlesnake
Rattling around!

Reptiles

Reptiles are crocodiles,
Turtles and snakes.
To be called a reptile
Here's what it takes:
Be a cold-blooded creature,
Have dry, scaly skin;
Breathe with your lungs,
Breathe out and breathe in.

Reptiles are alligators,
Tortoises, and lizards,
Hiding in the desert
From hot, sandy blizzards.
Some say that dinosaurs
Were reptiles long ago.
What is a reptile?
Well, now you know!

Rhinoceros

Did you ever see a rhinoceros nose?
Above its snout, a horn or two grows.
The horns can dig up bushes and trees.
They're strong, so the job is done with ease.
A rhino is proud of its horns, I suppose.
(It seems to take them wherever it goes!)
But though they are useful, I must disclose:
I'm thankful that *my* nose
Is not like the rhino's!

Robin

See the pretty robin,
Hear the robin sing.
Cheerful little robin,
First sign of spring!

Salamander

There's a salamander in that rotted old log.
It looks like a lizard, but it's more like a frog.
It likes to eat insects, it likes to eat bugs.
It likes to eat worms, and it likes to eat slugs.
The salamander's skin is slimy and black.
And when it loses its tail, another grows back!

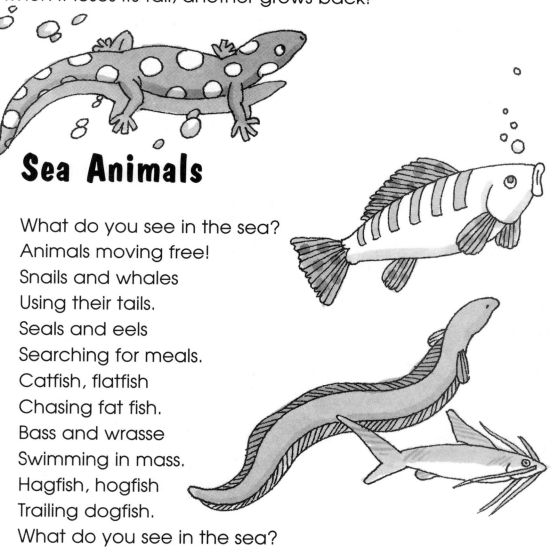

Sea Animals

What do you see in the sea?
Animals moving free!
Snails and whales
Using their tails.
Seals and eels
Searching for meals.
Catfish, flatfish
Chasing fat fish.
Bass and wrasse
Swimming in mass.
Hagfish, hogfish
Trailing dogfish.
What do you see in the sea?
Animals moving free!

Sea Horse

Can you ride a sea horse?
No, young boy!
It's tiny as a yoyo,
It's tiny as a toy!
Can you ride a sea horse?
No, young girl!
Its head looks like a horse
But its tail's a tiny curl.
Can you ride a sea horse?
No, though you may wish.
A sea horse is no *horse*, you see:
A sea horse is a *fish*!

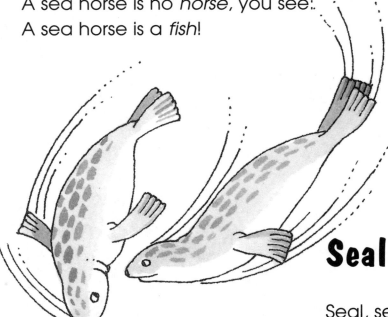

Seal

Seal, seal, in the sea,
Flapping flippers, swimming free.
Seal, seal, on the ice,
The whiskers on your lip are nice!
Seal, seal, in the zoo,
My seal of approval goes to you!

Shark

Shark teeth are sharp teeth,
A row above and a row beneath!
Shark skin is sharp skin,
With toothlike scales upon each fin!
A shark snout is a sharp snout,
A pointed nose that's sticking out!
Shark sense is a sharp sense,
Its sense of smell is most intense!
Shark fish are sharp fish,
So stay away where they splash and splish!

Sheep

Sheep are rather bashful,
Sheep are rather shy.
I asked a sheep the reason
But it wouldn't say why.

Shrimp

Have you ever seen a tiny shrimp?
It's less than an inch in size!
To see a teeny tiny shrimp
You may have to squint your eyes!

Silkworm

Silkworm, silkworm, white as milk,
How do you manage to make your silk?
Eating mulberry leaves all day,
Soon you're fat and on your way!
Now ready to spin your cocoon,
The cocoon is the silk, shining like the moon!
Silkworm, silkworm, white as milk,
Night and day, you make your silk!

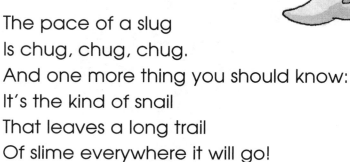

Skunk

Stink! Stank! Stunk!
I think I smell a skunk!
When it's upset, a skunk will spray
To keep its enemies far away.
The odor lasts for many a day!
Stink! Stank! Stunk!

Slug

What is a slug?
It isn't a bug.
It isn't a bird or a fish.
It's a kind of snail
That looks like a tail
And crawls in a sort of a swish.

The pace of a slug
Is chug, chug, chug.
And one more thing you should know:
It's the kind of snail
That leaves a long trail
Of slime everywhere it will go!

Snail

Slow as a snail,
That's what they say.
The snail slowly creeps along its way.
Snails in the desert,
Snails in the sea,
Snails in the forest crawling free.
Snails may be slow,
But this I've found:
Slowly but surely they get around!

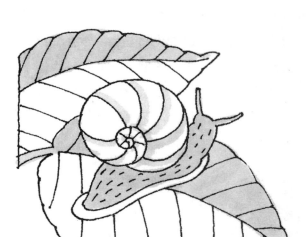

Snakes

For heaven's sake, so many snakes!
Garter snakes, cobras,
Milk snakes, rat snakes,
Copperheads, pythons,
Thin snakes, fat snakes!
King snakes, bull snakes,
Water snakes, tree snakes,
Vipers and rattlesnakes,
And many-more-to-see snakes!
For heaven's sake, so many snakes!!!

Spider

Spin, spider, spin!
Spin your web round and wide,
Spin your silky web with pride,
Greet the guests who come inside,
Spin, spider, spin!

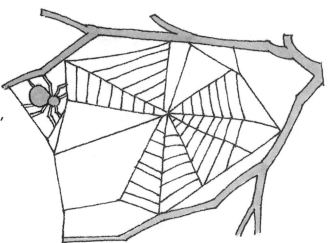

Squirrel

Watch the squirrel scamper,
Scamper on the ground.
The squirrel is busy storing nuts,
All the nuts it's found.

Watch the squirrel scamper,
Scamper up a tree.
The squirrel has a bushy tail
It's waving at me!

Watch the squirrel resting,
Resting in its den.
Eating all the nuts stored up
Until it's spring again!

Swan

Graceful on the water,
Graceful in the air,
Gliding oh, so gracefully
The swan is oh, so fair.

Graceful in the water,
Graceful in the sky,
Gliding oh, so gracefully
The swan is floating by.

Tiger

Some cats are big, and some cats are small,
But the tiger's the BIGGEST cat of all!
It's biggest in weight, it's biggest in length,
It's known for its beauty and known for its strength.

The tiger's coat is a bright orange-red.
Black stripes run from its tail to head.
The stripes blend in with the tall, tall grass,
So the tiger's not seen by those who pass.

Pounce! goes the tiger! Pounce! with a roar!
With teeth and claws you can't ignore!
Don't pet the tiger, for as you recall:
The tiger's the BIGGEST cat of all!

Turkey

Let's talk turkey!
What a walk it's got!
Strut about, strut about,
Do the turkey trot!

Let's talk turkey,
What a shaky wobble!
Strut about, strut about,
Gobble, gobble, gobble!

Turtle

Well, well, well,
Turtle in its shell!
On the land or in the sea,
Creeping slow or swimming free.
Crawling 'round on stubby legs,
Digging holes to lay its eggs.
Well, well, well,
Turtle in its shell!

Umbrella Bird

Have you ever heard
Of the umbrella bird?
It's really a bird, no jest!
High in a tree,
On its head you can see
A feathery umbrella-like crest!

Vicuna

Rub a vicuna's back
And you won't feel any bumps.
Though it's a type of camel,
A vicuna has no humps!

Walrus

The walrus is a very large seal,
And clams are its favorite meal.
On the ocean floor,
It searches for more,
And usually finds a great deal!

The walrus has tusks long and nice,
They help it to crawl on the ice.
If you had to be
Any seal in the sea,
A walrus would be my advice!

Wolf

Howl! cries the wolf!
Howl! Howl! Howl!
A lone little wolf
Is on the prowl.

Lost on the trail
Walking forward and back,
Looking for its family,
Looking for its pack.

Howl! cries the wolf!
Howl! Howl! Howl!
A lone little wolf
Is on the prowl.

Woodland Animals

Woodland animals live in the woods,
With plenty of trees in their neighborhoods.
The chipmunk, opossum, squirrel, and raccoon
Roam the woods all night and noon.
The bear and boar, the deer and moose,
All woodland creatures on the loose.
Near shores and ponds, and in the water
Are the beaver, muskrat, turtle, and otter.
Woodland animals are up in a tree,
The owl and koala you're sure to see.
Woodland animals like their view.
As a woodland creature, wouldn't you?

Woodpecker

Woodpecker, woodpecker,
Peck! Peck! Peck!
Drill with your bill
And bob your neck!

Peck out a hole
In the trunk of a tree.
Peck out a nest
For all to see.

Cling to the wood
With your sharp clawed feet.
Peck through the bark
And find bugs to eat!

Woodpecker, woodpecker,
Peck! Peck! Peck!
Drill with your bill
And bob your neck!

The World of Animals

Animals here, animals there,
Animal homes are everywhere!
High on a mountain slope so steep
Are the yak and panda, goat, and sheep.
In the grasslands, flat and wide,
The zebra and giraffe abide.
In woodland forests near the water
You'll find the bear and moose and otter.
In tropical forests with lots of rain
The toucan and the sloth remain.
Out in the desert hot and dry,
The camel and the snake go by.
In arctic regions filled with snow,
The polar bear and penguin go.
Deep in the ocean, a watery home,
The whale and shark and octopus roam.
Animals here, animals there,
Animal homes are everywhere!

Worm

Wiggle, wiggle, squiggle, squiggle,
Wiggly, squiggly worm.
With no backbone, with no legs,
How you twist and squirm!

Wiggle, wiggle, squiggle, squiggle,
All along the ground.
With your special sense of touch
You worm your way around!

Yak

Yak, yak, yak,
Yak, yak, yak.
If you talk to a yak,
Will it talk back?

Zebra

Black, white, black, white,
Black, white, black.
Stripes on the zebra
Front and back.

White, black, white, black,
White, black, white.
Stripes on the zebra
Left and right.

Animal Literature Links

Animal Literature Links

The following books about animals are suggested as further reading for children:

Bare, Colleen Stanley. *Busy, Busy Squirrels.* Dutton, New York, 1991.

Barrett, Judi. *Animals Should Definitely* Not *Wear Clothing,* illustrated by Ron Barrett. Aladdin, New York, 1988.

Borlenghi, Patricia. *From Albatross to Zoo.* Scholastic, New York, 1991.

Brett, Jan. *Annie and the Wild Animals.* Houghton Mifflin, New York, 1985.

_____. *The Mitten.* Putnam's Sons, New York, 1989.

Brown, Margaret Wise. *Where Have You Been?,* illustrated by Barbara Cooney. Hastings House, New York, 1952.

Carle, Eric. *The Mixed-Up Chameleon.* HarperCollins, New York, 1988.

Cole, Joanna. *Animal Sleepyheads: 1 to 10,* illustrated by Jeni Bassett. Scholastic, New York, 1988.

dePaola, Tomie. *The Kids' Cat Book.* Holiday House, New York, 1979.

Dorros, Arthur. *Animal Tracks.* Scholastic, New York, 1991.

Epstein, Sam and Beryl. *Bugs for Dinner?,* illustrated by Walter Gaffney-Kessell. Macmillan, New York, 1989.

Ehlert, Lois. *Feathers for Lunch.* Harcourt, San Diego, 1990.

Ets, Marie Hall. *In the Forest.* Viking, New York, 1944.

Ginsburg, Mirra. *Across the Stream,* illustrated by Nancy Tafuri. Puffin, New York, 1985.

Greenway, Shirley. *Animal Homes: Water.* Newington Press, Brookfield, CT, 1991.

Guarino, Deborah. *Is Your Mama a Llama?,* illustrated by Steven Kellogg. Scholastic, New York, 1989.

Heller, Ruth. *Animals Born Alive and Well.* Grosset & Dunlap, New York, 1982.

_____. *Chickens Aren't the Only Ones.* Grosset & Dunlap, New York, 1981.

Hepworth, Cathi. *Antics!* Putnam's Sons, New York, 1992.

Hirschi, Ron. *Who Lives in...the Alligator Swamp?*, Dodd, Mead, New York, 1987.

_____. *Where Are My Puppies, Whales, and Seals?*, photographs by Erwin and Peggy Bauer. Bantam, New York, 1992.

Jarrell, Randall. *The Animal Family*, illustrated by Maurice Sendak. Knopf, New York, 1987.

Kitchen, Bert. *Animal Alphabet.* Dial, New York, 1984.

_____. *Animal Numbers.* Dial, New York, 1987.

Kuchalla, Susan. *Baby Animals*, illustrated by Joel Snyder. Troll, Mahwah, N J, 1982.

_____. *Bears.* Troll, Mahwah, N J, 1982.

Leon, Dorothy. *One Eye, Two Eyes, Three Eyes, Four Eyes: The Many Ways Animals See.* Messner, New York, 1980.

Lionni, Leo. *Fish Is Fish.* Pantheon, New York, 1970.

Maris, Ron. *I Wish I Could Fly.* Greenwillow, New York, 1986.

McPhail, David. *Animals A to Z.* Scholastic, New York, 1988.

Numeroff, Laura Joffe. *If You Give a Mouse a Cookie*, illustrated by Felicia Bond. Harper & Row, New York, 1985.

Oppenheim, Joanna. *Have You Seen Birds?*, illustrated by Julio de Diego. Young Scott Books, New York, 1968.

Parker, N.W. and J.R. Wright *Frogs, Toads, Lizards, and Salamanders.* Greenwillow, New York, 1990.

Prelutsky, Jack. *Toucans Two and Other Poems*, illustrated by Jose Aruego. Macmillan, New York, 1970.

Royston, Angela. *What's Inside? Shells*, illustrated by Richard Manning. Dorling Kindersley, New York, 1991.

Ryder, Joanne. *The Snail's Spell*, illustrated by Lynne Cherry. Viking, New York, 1982.

_____. *Lizard in the Sun*, illustrated by Michael Rothman. Morrow, New York, 1990.

Singer, Marilyn. *Turtle in July*, illustrated by Jerry Pickney. Macmillan, New York, 1989.

Tongren, Sally. *What's for Lunch?: Animal Feeding at the Zoo.* Galison, New York, 1981.

Wadsworth, Olive A. *Over in the Meadow*, illustrated by David Carter. Scholastic, New York, 1992.

Whipple, Laura. *Eric Carle's Animals, Animals*, illustrated by Eric Carle. Philomel, New York, 1989.

Wormell, Christopher. *An Alphabet of Animals.* Dial, New York, 1990.

Yoshida, Toshi. *Young Lions.* Philomel, New York, 1989.

The following books about animals are suggested as further reading for the teacher:

Bender, Lionel. *Animals of the Night.* Gloucester Press, New York, 1989.

Chinery, Michael. *All About Baby Animals*, illustrated by Ian Jackson. Doubleday, New York, 1989.

Dewey, Jennifer Owings. *Animal Architecture.* Orchard Books, New York, 1991.

Doubilet, Anne. *Under the Sea From A to Z*, photographs by David Doubilet. Crown, New York, 1991.

Hadden, Sue. *Weird and Wonderful Insects.* Thomson Learning, New York, 1993.

Kudlinski, Kathleen. *Animal Tracks & Traces*, illustrated by Mary Morgan. Franklin Watts, New York, 1991.

Littlejohn, Claire. *The Modern Ark: The Endangered Wildlife of Our Planet.* Dial, New York, 1990.

Sattler, Helen Roney. *Fish Facts & Bird Brains*, illustrated by Giulio Maestro. Lodestar, New York, 1984.

Selsam, Millicent. *How Animals Live Together.* Morrow, New York, 1979.

Taylor, Barbara. *The Animal Atlas*, illustrated by Kenneth Lilly. Knopf, New York, 1992.